CRUISIN'

RVs and Vans

By Stephen Burt

PUBLISHED BY

Capstone Press

Mankato, Minnesota USA

CIP
LIBRARY OF CONGRESS CATALOGING IN
PUBLICATION DATA

Burt, Stephen
      Rvs and vans / by Stephen Burt.
           p. cm. — (Cruisin')
      Summary: Discusses recreational vehicles and vans: their
      design, who uses them, and why they are important to
      their owners.

      ISBN 1-56065-071-0
      1. Recreational vehicles—Juvenile literature. 2. Vans—
      Juvenile literature. [1. Recreational vehicles. 2. Vans.]
      I. Title. II. Series.
      TL298.B87   1989
      629.226—dc20   89-25230
                                    CIP
                                    AC

Photo Credit:
Diarama 3, 4, 6, 16, 18, 20, 25, 38, 39, 40, 48

Pleasure Land Company 9, 10, 12, 13, 14, 15, 41, 44

Val VanDenberg 17, 19, 21, 22, 23, 24, 26 27 30, 31, 32, 33, 34, 35, 36, 37

Ford 28, 29

Steve Datnoff 43, 45

Capstone Press
P.O. Box 669, Mankato, MN, U.S.A. 56002-0669

CONTENTS

ON THE OPEN ROAD

Are you interested in the open road? Do you like to go to the seashore, the mountains, or the sunny South, or just spend time outdoors?

If you are traveling on the open road, you will need a **recreational vehicle**. Recreational vehicles, or **RVs**, come in several different types, but they all carry equipment for living while out traveling. The largest ones are like moveable homes. People called **full-timers** live in them all year round.

The earliest RVs were converted trucks. Henry Ford, the inventor and car maker, built a camping truck complete with a refrigerator. He even took the President along on a trip in 1921. The first mass-produced camping trailers actually appeared in the 1930's. Some had beds, kitchens, a water supply, and electric lights. The one-piece **motor homes** common today came on the scene in the 1960's. By 1985, over seven million American households owned an RV.

In this book, you will learn about the different kinds of RVs and how they are used. Then you will understand why RVs are so popular, and why more and more people are discovering adventures on the open road.

TYPES OF RECREATIONAL VEHICLES

There are four types of RVs. They are motor homes, RV vans, trailers, and pickup campers. Each type has a different size and shape.

Motor Homes

A motor home is a type of RV which is a **complete unit**. A complete unit means that the engine and driver's seat are in the same area as the living space. Passengers can bring the driver cold drinks from the refrigerator without going outside. Travelling in a motor home is fun and very comfortable. There are also different kinds of motor homes.

Class A Motor Homes - Class A motor homes range from 20 to 40 feet long. The largest ones look like very fancy buses. They can cost up to $350,000, or about the same as the cost of 20 cars. Most cost between $50,000 and $125,000.

The **chassis** of a Class A motor home needs to be very strong. These motor homes can weigh up to 35,000 pounds. That is more than the weight of ten cars. Because of the size of these vehicles, their engines are large.

Class A motor home.

Inside a Class A motor home.

The roof of a Class A is over ten feet high. This can be too tall for the motor home to go under some railway and highway underpasses. Drivers need to watch for height restrictions as they travel.

Inside, the motor home is finished to look like a miniature house. It is very comfortable inside, with air conditioning and heating. The space is carpeted and paneled. Usually there is a living room plus a kitchen and dining area, and a bathroom complete with a shower. These vehicles also have built-in TVs, stereos, microwaves, and even VCRs.

The Class A RV can be independent of outside power and water for long periods of time. It carries its own **electrical generator** to provide electricity, and large tanks for fresh and dirty water.

Many owners of these large RVs tow a car behind or include bicycles. After parking the RV, they drive the car or use the bike to run errands and explore the area.

Mini-Motor Homes - The mini-motor home is built on a van chassis supplied by an automaker. The motor home manufacturer buys the chassis and converts it into a motor home between 20 and 30 feet long.

You can recognize a mini-motor home because of its shape. The front end looks like a pickup or a van. A section of the RV body often overhangs the driver's cab. This area usually holds a bed, but it sometimes serves as a storage space.

The weight of the average mini-motor home is more than 6,500 pounds. Most weigh about 10,000 pounds, and cost between $30,000 and $60,000. Because they are smaller and lighter, they use smaller engines that are located in the front.

Inside a mini-motor home is very comfortable.

The mini-motor home provides many of the same facilities and features as the Class A motor homes. The mini-motor home is built from the same materials as the Class A, and it too can travel on its own. It has less room inside, but it is less expensive to buy. Fuel costs are also less because it is lighter. The smaller size makes it easier to maneuver and park.

The mini-motor home makes a day at the amusement park a fun event.

Micro-mini Motor Home - The micro-mini motor home is a smaller version of the mini-motor home. It has the same shape, and it is built on the chassis of a light pickup truck or a van. The micro-mini weighs less than 6,500 pounds.

Micro-minis need to be light, since they have small engines for better fuel economy. If they are heavily loaded they climb slowly uphill.

The micro-mini has lots of room inside for special guests or purchases.

The cost of a micro-mini ranges between $20,000 and $35,000. Many features, like TVs and refrigerators, are available the same as for the large motor homes. However, as the RVs get smaller, the space inside shrinks. Equipment needs to be stowed away or folded up. The seats and table used for dining usually change into a bed for sleeping.

The mini-motor home and the micro-mini motor home have lower roofs than the Class A motor home. They are able to park in more places and their drivers do not have to watch for low overhead clearances.

Inside the micro-mini is compact but offers lots of extras.

RV Vans

Wide Body Vans - Wide body vans are constructed on a van chassis. They have roofs that are much lower than the micro-mini motor homes. The wide body flares out behind the cab and gives more room for a living area than in regular vans.

The wide body van has many of the same comforts as the mini-motor home. It is also almost as expensive. The wide body van does not provide as much headroom inside for storage and does not have room for a loft bed. However, it can be parked in most garages and is as easy to drive as a car.

The wide body van can be parked in most parking lots.

Van Campers - Van campers are built from panel trucks. A van camper may be fitted with sleeping, kitchen, and toilet facilities. It may have a raised roof for a sleeping loft or storage. The price of a van camper ranges from $20,000 to $40,000.

The van camper can be used for a weekend campout or a cross-country vacation.

Trailers

Trailers are not complete units like motor homes. They do not have their own engines and require the trailer and a **tow vehicle** to pull it. Many people choose a trailer as an RV because it has the most living space. A trailer can also be parked and disconnected from the towing car.

There are drawbacks to trailers. A trailer is harder to drive, especially when backing up. There are also additional costs of more tires and insurance. A car

A trailer can be unhitched from the towing vehicle. The family has transportation for sight-seeing or to get supplies.

pulling a trailer needs more parking space. On the road, people cannot move back and forth between the trailer and the car. Many states will not allow people to ride inside the trailer while it is being towed.

Travel Trailers - The travel trailer is a popular RV trailer. It is 12 to 35 feet long, and weighs up to 8,000 pounds. Some have **tandem axles**, two axles placed close together whose wheels share the trailer's weight. This trailer is too heavy to be towed by most cars. It requires a strong vehicle such as a van, pickup, or truck.

Lightweight Travel Trailers - This RV trailer is designed to be pulled by most cars or light pickup trucks. It weighs from 800 to 2,000 pounds and is easier to tow. Even though it is small, the lightweight travel trailer has room for cooking, eating, and sleeping.

This lightweight trailer lets the traveler cook right at the lake and provides a comfortable way to wait for the rain to stop.

Fifth Wheel Trailers - A heavy-duty pickup or truck tows the fifth wheel trailer. The truck's hitch is carried over its rear axle, in its bed, rather than near the bumper. The front end of the trailer is raised to go over, or overlap, the rear of the truck. The fifth wheel trailer is very securely hooked and is more maneuverable.

The fifth wheel trailer varies widely in weight and size. It can be between 20 and 50 feet long, and weigh between 5,000 and 15,000 pounds. Prices range from $12,000 to $70,000. A larger one has complete bed, living, kitchen, and bathroom areas.

The fifth wheel trailer at Kootenay National Park, B.C.

Fold-down Camping Trailers - Camping trailers are often a family's first step in RVs. On the road, the trailer folds into a low box. At the campsite, the top of the trailer is raised. A tent pops up, with wings at the ends. Inside the wings are large beds. In the center is room for a stove, sink, and table. Some camping trailers have small heaters for chilly days.

The camping trailer is light and easy to tow. It can be pulled behind a family car using an ordinary trailer hitch. Compared with other RVs, its cost is low. At home, folded up, the camping trailer can be stored conveniently in a garage or a corner of the driveway.

Camping trailer at the campsite while the family is sightseeing.

Pickup Campers

The pickup camper is actually a living space mounted on the back of a pickup truck. The camper can be taken off and left standing on stilts when it is not needed.

The pickup camper has room for three to six people. Inside are small cooking, eating, and sleeping areas. The pickup camper is often used by people who hunt or fish, since they spend most of their time outdoors and stay in the camper only at night.

Here the pickup camper will provide cooking and sleeping accommodations once the fishermen finish for the day.

A pickup camper can make a quick roadside stop for lunch or a short break.

This van provides lots of comfortable seating for a fishing crew.

Vans

The world of vans is changing very quickly. More and more people are discovering how useful vans can be.

A van is simply a box on top of a truck or light pickup chassis. In the basic van, there is no partition between the driver's area and the rest of the van. Vans are popular because they have lots of conveniences and space for their small size.

Now here's a van that really is useful.

TYPES OF VANS

Cargo and Commercial Vans - These vans usually have no windows in their sides and are used to carry tools, equipment, or materials for a business.

The smaller cargo van is good for deliveries of small items, like flowers and small packages. The larger commercial van hauls larger, heavier items. A plumber can carry many different lengths of pipe and heavy tools in his commercial van. The cargo or commercial van is easy to park and drive.

Passenger Vans - The passenger van has windows on the sides and in the back. The number and kind of seats installed in the van determines the number of passengers. Bench seats, which are like school bus seats, hold the most people. Individual seats do not provide as much seating space but are more comfortable.

The 1992 Aerostar is perfect to run a group to the ball game, and it provides comfort on a long trip.

A large van with bench seats carries up to 15 passengers. Many vans have removeable seats to make space for cargo or luggage. For another trip, the seats can be put back to haul more people.

The passenger van is popular with many families. A passenger van takes groups on outings or to summer camp. A specially equipped passenger van can be used to carry handicapped people. Airport transportation companies use passenger vans with bench seats.

The 1992 Econo Club Wagon can carry up to 15 people at one time!

Conversion Vans - A bare, unfinished van changed into a comfortable, finished, travel van is called a conversion van.

Makers of conversion vans are known as converters. Converters take an unfinished commercial or passenger van from the factory and install windows, insulation, carpeting, and other special features like a sound system, TV, and snack tables. Some conversion van seats change into bed space. There also may be a cooler for drinks and snacks. Some vans have ladders on the back, or a luggage carrier on the roof. Chrome and bright colors decorate the outside of the conversion van.

This conversion van has provided busy shoppers with a comfortable trip to the mall.

Conversion vans fit right into regular parking spaces.

Custom Vans - The word *custom* means "made to order." Every custom van differs from the next one. Each one is made to order for one person. The custom van shows the imagination of its owner.

The custom van starts as a new or used commercial van. The owner chooses the special features for the inside and the color for the outside. Owners often do the work themselves. Custom vans can be used either to show or for regular traveling. The show van is designed for appearance, or for show. It displays bright

This new van is waiting for an owner to make it into a custom van.

and elaborate paint finishes. Hundreds of hours of work go into finely detailed pictures and designs making up the finish. This van is not driven on the street every day. It is taken to special meets, where it competes with other vans to see which is judged the best.

The go or cruising van is meant to be used. It can include such features as a folding bed, a refrigerator, an expensive stereo. The cruising van may also have custom-built driver and passenger seats. Often, over-size wheels and chrome exhaust pipes finish off the special outside appearance.

Minivans - *Mini* means "small." This is the smallest van. It is part car and part van. The driver sits up high, but this little van drives like a car. The minivan fits into a regular car's space. The minivan is rapidly becoming the most popular kind of family van. New models appear every year. Most minivans have windows all around and can carry up to seven passengers. A large side door slides open to let passengers in and out.

The minivan is perfect for families. Child seats fit easily and are now being built into some of the newer models. The rear seats also can be removed to make more room. Around town, the minivan carries people and groceries. On vacation, there is room for everyone as well as the luggage. Many minivans can be used to tow a small trailer or boat.

The minivan is as easy as a car to use. It offers less space and power than a full-size van. The minivan works best for people who need a combination of both vehicles.

RV LIFE

Planning the Trip

The fun of an RV is the many places to visit. Do you want to swim at the seashore, or hike in the mountains? Do you want to watch wildlife, or meet Mickey Mouse? The choice is up to you.

Visiting a national park in a wide body van includes the family pets.

Books printed especially for RVers list all types of campgrounds and RV parks. The books list all of the facilities available, from picnic tables and fire grates to golf courses and video arcades. The campground description even tells what natural features are in the area.

Every state has a department of tourism. If you write to these departments for information about the states you want to visit, you will receive packets of information about places of special interest, museums, and places to camp with your RV. RVers also read magazines written especially for them. Articles in the magazines describe trips other RVers have taken and tell about the attractions they have seen.

This motor home is traveling on the Oregon Coast.

On the Road

Traveling in one of the larger RVs can be slower than in a car or in one of the smaller versions of the RV. On mountains, the larger RV may need to pull over to let other vehicles go by. If the RV is a large Class A, it can be swayed by winds, making it necessary to go slower. A good RV driver avoids problems by being cautious.

In an RV, going slower does not always mean getting there later. While the other vehicles need to stop for lunch, the RV just keeps going. It might even end up ahead at the end of the day.

Sight-seeing in Monument Valley, Utah, in a motor home.

Camping

RV campgrounds may be private or public. Private campgrounds usually have stores and laundries, and some even have amusement areas. Public campgrounds, located in state and national parks, may have more natural settings, with forests and wildlife.

At the entrance to the campground, the RVers choose a camping spot. Trailers and large motor homes might want a **pull-through**. The RV can enter and leave a pull-through site by driving ahead in a loop.

If one of the larger RVs needs to back up, it is necessary to have someone stand behind the RV and direct the driver using hand signals. Today, the more expensive motor homes have a video camera mounted at the back. The driver looks at a video screen beside his seat to see what is behind the RV.

After finding a camping spot, the RV needs to be leveled. RV refrigerators work best when the RV is parked evenly. Sometimes people level the RV by putting some of the wheels on ramps or planks. Many of the RVs level themselves by computer.

Most of the private campgrounds have **RV hookups** with an electrical outlet and a water faucet. The RV hooks up to the water, and a heavy electrical cord plugs the RV into the campground's outlet. The RVer also attaches a hose that carries fresh water to the RV's water system. As long as the RV stays in the site, it is supplied with water and electricity through the hookups.

KOA in Hammond, Oregon.

CLUBS AND ORGANIZATIONS

Many people who own RVs join clubs. The clubs schedule rallies or get-togethers. RVers come from great distances to attend. They look forward to seeing old friends and making new ones.

Sometimes RVers meet in order to take an organized trip together. This is called "caravaning." The RVs travel in a planned order, switching places in the line from day to day. The front and back RVs communicate by radio.

Visiting antique shops in a micro-mini.

A travel trailer on the open road north of Spences Bridge, B.C.

GLOSSARY

Chassis: the frame of a vehicle

Complete unit: an RV that has driving and living space in one vehicle

Electrical generator: motor that makes electricity

Full-timers: people who live in their RVs all year

Motor home: more fully equipped RVs that are like a home on wheels

Pull-through: camping site RVs use without backing up

Recreational vehicle: travel vehicle suitable for living on the road

RV: short for Recreational Vehicle

RV hookups: connection for water and electricity at RV campsites

Tandem axles: axles placed closely behind one another to share the weight of a vehicle

Tow vehicle: truck, van, or pickup that pulls a camping trailer

INDEX

RVs camping at Maryhill State Park in Washington.